THE POCKET Whisky

Published in 2026
by Gemini Gift Books
Part of Gemini Books Group

Based in Woodbridge and London

Marine House, Tide Mill Way,
Woodbridge, Suffolk IP12 1AP
United Kingdom

www.geminibooks.com

Part of the Gemini Pockets series

Text by Laura Gladwin
Cover illustration by Clare Owen

ISBN 978-1-80247-349-0

A CIP catalogue record for this book is available from the British Library.

Manufacturer's EU Representative: Eurolink Compliance Limited,
25 Herbert Place, Dublin, D02 AY86, Republic of Ireland.
admin@eurolink-europe.ie

Printed in China

10 9 8 7 6 5 4 3 2 1

Picture Credits: Picture credits: Shutterstock: 4, 7, 34 / ECE design; 12, 16, 22, 88, 95, 117 / Qualit Design; 26 / Istry Istry; 32, 95 / MoreVector; 98, 121 / Epine; 103, 104 / Vectorgoods studio; 109 / Victoria Sergeeva; 111 / kridoarts; 123 / Sketch Master. Freepik: 8, 40; 84 / RawPixel.

THE POCKET

Whisky

CONTENTS

INTRODUCTION

Whisky has enthralled lovers of strong drink for centuries, whether sipped from cut-glass tumblers by true connoisseurs or swigged from the bottle by campfire revellers. Its amber glow, warming quality and intricate flavours give it a mystique of its own. Its ingredients may be humble – ordinary grain, yeast and water – but much of the flavour alchemy comes from the skill of the blender and distiller, and years-long maturation in wooden casks.

With its origins firmly in Scotland and Ireland in the 15th century, there are now many styles across the globe, as makers put their own contemporary twist on *uisge beatha*, or the "water of life".

From the historic heartlands of the amber liquor to modern distillation methods, we explore the story of whisky, and how to best enjoy a dram or two along the way.

Chapter One

Whisky 101

All About the Dram

"Freedom and whisky gang thegither."

Robert Burns,
***The Author's Earnest Cry and Prayer* (1786)**

WHAT IS WHISKY?

Whisky is a spirit made from grain, usually barley, rye, wheat or corn. Single malt and blended are the classic varieties of Scotch whisky. American whiskeys such as bourbon use corn and rye.

The prepared grain is mixed with water to create a "mash". This is fermented into a beer-like liquid called the "wash", which is distilled, aged in casks and then blended to create the final product.

The characteristics of the finished product depend on the mix of grains, how they are prepared, the length of ageing and what wood is used, and the selection of whiskies for the final blend.

THE RAW MATERIALS

Grain

The grain is malted: soaked, allowed to germinate and then heated in order to extract sugar for fermentation.

Yeast

Yeast is added to the ground-up malted grain to begin fermentation.

Water

Whisky-making requires lots of water. It's sometimes claimed that the type of water used is crucial for the taste of the final product. In fact, it probably doesn't make a huge difference.

THE DISTILLATION PROCESS

Once the malt and grains have been fermented into a beer (called wash), distillation is carried out. The wash is boiled to produce alcoholic vapours, which are then condensed into spirit. This is done in large vessels known as stills. The design of the stills influences the flavour of the spirit produced.

Most whiskies are double distilled: there's a first distillation followed by a second stage that increases the alcohol content. During the second stage, different compounds are released. The "heart" of the spirit – the most desirable part of the distillate produced in the middle of the process – is reserved for the final whisky. Compounds produced at the start and end of the distillation (the "heads" and the "tails") are discarded.

THE ORIGINS OF *UISGE BEATHA*

The word "whisky" is derived from the Gaelic for "water of life" – *uisge beatha* – and has roots in 15th-century Ireland and Scotland. Initially, whisky wasn't aged, which meant that early versions were much rawer and fierier than today's drink.

The introduction of the column still in the 19th century sped up the process of distillation, allowing for higher production volumes. Whiskey (with an e) making emerged in America when Scottish and Irish settlers began distilling it, creating their own versions of the drink, such as bourbon.

SCOTTISH WHISKY REGIONS

Highland
Scotland's largest whisky region, covering the north and the western isles, produces many varieties from light to full-bodied.

Speyside
Whiskies from Speyside in the north east are smooth and fruity.

Campbeltown
Whiskies from Campbeltown in the south west have rich notes of fruit, smoke and salt.

Islay
Whiskies from this large Hebridean island have strong flavours of peat and smoke.

Lowland
Lowland whiskies tend to be lighter without peaty notes.

WHISKY'S QUEST FOR WORLD DOMINATION

Today, whisky is made all over the world, from Scotland to South Africa, and Japan to New Zealand.

There are significant emerging markets for whisky in India and Southeast Asia.

PEATED WHISKY

Malting involves the toasting of barley, and in Scotland it has been traditional to use peat as the fuel to do this. It's the phenol compounds in the peat smoke that give peated whiskies their distinctive smoky flavour profile; the more peat used in the roasting process, the more this comes through.

Peat is harvested from bogs, and is therefore an important part of a whisky's terroir (the environmental factors that give whisky its distinctive character). Laphroaig is a famous peated whisky distilled on Islay in Scotland.

WHISKY OR WHISKEY?

Traditionally, whisky is spelled without the "e" in Scotland, Canada and Japan, and with an "e" in Ireland and America.

Some producers will depart from this tradition to indicate that their liquor is made in the classic Scottish style (whisky) or in the sweeter American bourbon style (whiskey).

TOP 10 WORLDWIDE MARKETS FOR WHISKY

India

USA

UK

France

Japan

Germany

Canada

Australia

Spain

Mexico

The most expensive whiskey ever made is the Emerald Isle from The Craft Irish Whiskey Co., a limited edition of only seven bottles, one of which sold for $2.8 million in 2024.

Aged for 30 years in rare casks, the whiskey comes with a green and white Fabergé egg containing an uncut emerald.

TYPES OF WHISKY

Single Malt: A malt whisky from a single distillery.

Single Cask: A whisky bottled from just one cask (single malts can be blended from different casks).

Blended Scotch: A whisky created from a blend of different whiskies.

Bourbon Whiskey: An American whiskey made predominantly with corn.

Tennessee Whiskey: Similar to bourbon, but with the addition of a charcoal filtration process.

Rye Whiskey: Made with rye grain and aged in oak barrels.

Sour Mash Whiskey: An American-style whiskey in which some of the solids from the previous batch of fermented grain are kept in to kickstart fermentation.

MALT OR GRAIN?

Malt whiskies are made from malted barley, while grain whiskies include other grains such as wheat, corn or rye. Single malts and single grains come from a single distillery.

Blended malts are made from single malts from more than one distillery, while blended grains are a mixture of different single grains. Blended Scotch whisky consists of both single malts and single grains, with the malts supplying the stronger flavours.

THE WHISKY STOCK EXCHANGE

People invest in whisky as they do in stocks and shares. One way of doing this is to buy a cask of whisky. As the whisky matures, the value of the cask should rise, allowing the investor to make a profit.

Collectors also buy and sell rare or limited-edition bottles. Once whisky is bottled, it stops maturing, so profit has to come from picking a bottle that is highly collectible.

AMERICAN WHISKEYS

American whiskey-making began when European settlers applied their distillation skills to the abundant crops of the emerging nation. In the 1700s, bourbon production began in Kentucky.

Late in the century, the Whiskey Rebellion arose in protest at a tax on the spirit. With 1920s Prohibition, many distilleries closed, but afterwards, American whiskey-making re-emerged and grew into today's thriving global industry.

Bourbon is made with at least 51 per cent corn, giving it a sweet flavour.

Rye whiskey is made with at least 51 per cent rye and has a spicy, often peppery taste.

Rye malt whiskey is made with malted rye, making it richer than unmalted rye.

Wheat whiskey is a less common but smooth and easy-drinking tipple.

Corn whiskey is made from at least 80 percent corn and is sweet, but tends to be lighter than bourbon.

"**Kentucky straight**" means that the whiskey has been made in Kentucky following specific rules, such as having been aged for at least two years in charred oak barrels.

AGE STATEMENTS

The flavour and colour of whisky comes from ageing it in wood barrels, hence the age statements given on the bottles.

A blended whisky may contain several whiskies of different ages.

If it's a ten-year-old blend, then the youngest whisky in it is ten years old.

As whisky matures in the cask, a small amount of it evaporates into the air.

Traditionally, this has been called the "angel's share" – the portion of it that's said to be consumed by the angels.

TYPES OF STILL

Pot stills

The traditional kind of still, this is a large copper vessel that is heated to produce vapour. A pipe takes the vapour into a condenser. Pot distillation helps preserve flavour.

Column stills

These are columns that allow continuous distillation (rather than in batches as in pot stills). They allow for the faster production of spirit with a high alcohol content, but create less richness.

WHO'S WHO OF WHISKY

The **maltster** selects the barley and carries out the malting process.

The **mashman** mixes malt with hot water to create the mash.

The **master distiller** oversees the entire process of distillation.

The **cooper** makes and maintains the wooden barrels used to age the whisky.

The **blender** creates the final whisky by blending different batches of whisky together.

WHISKY TOURISM

The growing popularity of whisky has made whisky tourism big business. Whisky trails are a great way of learning about the history of the spirit, tasting the local whiskies as well as taking in beautiful scenery along the way.

The Malt Whisky Trail in Scotland covers the Speyside region, where you can visit distilleries including Benromach and Glenlivet.

For American whiskey fans, the Kentucky Bourbon Trail features makers such as Jim Beam and Maker's Mark.

The oldest licensed whiskey distillery in the world is Bushmills in Northern Ireland, whose origins go back to 1608.

IRISH WHISKEY

Irish whiskey is made from barley and other grains, often using triple distillation, which helps give the variety its classic light, smooth taste with hints of fruit. These whiskeys tend not to have the smoky, peaty flavours associated with Scotch whiskies.

Irish whiskeys include single malts, grain whiskeys and blended whiskeys.

CANADIAN WHISKY

The regulations governing the production of whisky are looser in Canada than in some other places. Pretty much any mix of grains can be used, though Canadian whisky is particularly associated with rye.

Any type of oak barrel may be used and there are no geographical restrictions, but it must be aged for a minimum of three years.

Canadian whiskies often have a flavour profile similar to Scotch blends. Well-known brands include Crown Royal and Canadian Club.

JAPANESE WHISKY

Commercial whisky distilling began in Japan in the 1920s, when the founder of the country's industry, Masataka Taketsuru, returned home from studying at Glasgow University with a passion for Scotch and a desire to recreate it.

Japanese whisky is rooted in the Scotch style, but Japan has made that tradition its own.

The country is now a major whisky player, exporting celebrated brands around the world. Japan's two leading whisky producers are Suntory and Nikka.

AUSTRALIAN WHISKY

Whisky distilling in Australia goes back to the 19th century, but underwent a renaissance in the 1990s with the emergence of innovative craft whisky companies producing in small batches.

Tasmania is a leading region, with a cooler climate ideal for whisky production. The country's varied climate allows for the production of many styles of whiskies, and the use of local grains and woods for casks create unique flavour profiles.

OTHER WHISKY-PRODUCING COUNTRIES

Austria

Belgium

Denmark

England

Finland

France

Germany

India

Italy

Mexico

Netherlands

New Zealand

Norway

South Africa

Spain

Sweden

Switzerland

Wales

THE WHISKEY PRAYER

This traditional poem celebrates
whiskey in the Irish tradition.

**"May the road rise
up to meet you,**

**May the wind be
always at your back,**

**May the sun shine
warm upon your face,**

**And may a bottle of
whiskey always be
within reach."**

WHISKY BARRELS

The spirit that comes out of the still is clear – not yet proper whisky. What gives the colour and complex flavours to the final product is the process of maturation in wooden casks.

Oak is the most common barrel type, with European oak giving rich, fruity flavours.

Bourbon gets its sweetness partly from being aged in brand new and charred casks. Used bourbon barrels are commonly reused by Irish and Scottish whisky producers.

WHISKY SPIN-OFFS

Baileys Irish Cream: A sweet liqueur of Irish whiskey, cocoa and cream.

Drambuie: A Scotch-based liqueur made with heather honey, herbs and spices. Can be drunk on its own or in cocktails.

Southern Comfort: A sweet, fruity American whiskey-based liqueur flavoured with peach and spices.

Glayva: Rich and warming, Glayva, meaning "very good" in Gaelic, combines flavours of tangerine, honey and cinnamon with Scotch whisky.

Jim Beam Honey: The famous bourbon combined with honey, giving a smooth, sweet sipping experience.

Chapter Two

Whiskies Around the World

Bottles to Look Out For

“The light music of whisky falling into glasses made an agreeable interlude.”

James Joyce, *Dubliners* (1914)

SCOTLAND

Aberfeldy

Location: Perthshire, Scottish Highlands

Key facts:

Only available as single malts, Aberfeldy whisky is also used in Dewars blended Scotch.

It's known as the Golden Dram, thanks to the gold deposits found in the local area, and is characterized by balanced dried fruit, gentle smoke and citrus.

Bottles to look out for:

18-year-old Aberfeldy (ABV 43%)
21-year-old Aberfeldy (ABV 40%)

SCOTLAND

Balvenie

Location: Dufftown, Morayshire

Key facts:

Balvenie is one of the few distilleries in Scotland to carry out traditional malting in-house using local peat.

The distillery also has its own cooperage for the making of barrels.

Its single malts are finished in a variety of casks, including European oak sherry casks, giving its whiskies rich and complex flavour layers.

Bottles to look out for:

12-year-old Doublewood (ABV 40%)
16-year-old French Oak (ABV 47.6%)

SCOTLAND

Benromach

Location: Forres, Morayshire

Key facts:

A traditional Speyside distillery, Benromach reopened in 1998 after many years of closure.

It employs locally grown barley and spring water from the nearby Romach Hills to produce its lightly peated single malt, with notes of sherry, vanilla and orange.

Bottles to look out for:

10-year-old Benromach (ABV 43%)
21-year-old Benromach (ABV 43%)

SCOTLAND

Bowmore

Location: Islay, Hebrides

Key facts:

The first distillery on Islay, Bowmore was established in 1779 and still makes its own malted barley using traditional methods.

The distillery is known for its smoky, sherried single malts with notes of tropical fruit and delicate spice.

Bottles to look out for:

12-year-old Bowmore (ABV 49%)
18-year-old Bowmore (ABV 43%)

SCOTLAND

Glenfiddich

Location: Dufftown, Morayshire

Key facts:

A family-owned distillery famous for its Speyside single malts and triangular bottle, which represents the three ingredients of Glenfiddich's whiskies: water, yeast and malted barley.

Glenfiddich whiskies can be delicately fruity, and rich and spicy.

Bottles to look out for:

12-year-old Glenfiddich (ABV 40%)
21-year-old Gran Reserva (ABV 40%)

SCOTLAND

Glenlivet

Location: Ballindalloch, Morayshire

Key facts:

Beginning as an illegal distillery in the early nineteenth century, Glenlivet once produced whiskies mainly for blending but is now one of the major single malt players.

Made with unpeated malt, Glenlivet whiskies are renowned for their light, fruity style.

Bottles to look out for:

12-year-old Double Oak (ABV 40%)
14-year-old Single Cask Butt (ABV 61.9%)

SCOTLAND

Glenmorangie

Location: Tain, Highlands

Key facts:

In operation since 1843, the Glenmorangie distillery has the tallest copper pot stills in Scotland.

It is famous for its unpeated single malts with smooth, fruity flavours and hints of vanilla and honey.

Bottles to look out for:

12-year-old Glenmorangie (ABV 40%)
18-year-old Glenmorangie (ABV 43%)

SCOTLAND

Glen Moray

Location: Elgin, Morayshire

Key facts:

The Speyside distillery of Glen Moray uses traditional copper stills and has become known for experimenting with a wide variety of casks for ageing its whiskies.

It was one of the first to use white wine casks and has also used sherry and port casks, lending its whiskies a wide range of flavour profiles.

Bottles to look out for:

18-year-old Glen Moray (ABV 47.2%)
21-year-old Portwood Finish (ABV 46.3%)

SCOTLAND

Glen Scotia

Location: Campbeltown, Argyll

Key facts:

A historic distillery that produces peated and unpeated single malt.

In the nineteenth century, its single malts were in high demand by producers of blended whisky.

Today, its whiskies represent the classic Campbeltown style, with complex notes of brine, fruit and smoke.

Bottles to look out for:

9-year-old Festival Edition 2025 (ABV 54.3%)
18-year-old Glen Scotia (ABV 46%)

SCOTLAND

Kilchoman

Location: Islay, Hebrides

Key facts:

Established in 2005 at Rockside Farm on the west coast of Islay, Kilchoman was the first new distillery on the island for over a century.

Its 100 per cent Islay series uses barley from Rockside Farm only, with every stage of production done on site.

Its single malts combine peat smoke with crisp citrus and rich spice.

Bottles to look out for:

100% Islay (ABV 50%)
Machir Bay (ABV 46%)

SCOTLAND

Springbank

Location: Campbeltown, Argyll

Key facts:

A family-owned distillery that dates back to the early nineteenth century and employing traditional production methods, the celebrated Springbank single malt is double distilled and lightly peated, with notes of rhubarb and mango and a smoky finish.

The distillery also produces the more heavily peated whisky, Longrow, as well as the triple-distilled Hazelburn.

Bottles to look out for:

10-year-old Springbank (ABV 46%)
Longrow Peated (ABV 46%)

SCOTLAND

Talisker

Location: Isle of Skye, Hebrides

Key facts:

The oldest working distillery on the Isle of Skye, Talisker is located on the shores of Loch Harport, and its peated single malts have a distinctly coastal character with notes of brine and seaweed alongside spice and fruit.

Talisker now comes under the Diageo portfolio as one of its Six Classic Malts of Scotland.

Bottles to look out for:

10-year-old Talisker (ABV 45.8%)
18-year-old Talisker (ABV 56.2%)

NORTHERN IRELAND

Bushmills

Location: County Antrim

Key facts:

The Old Bushmills Distillery was founded in 1784 and is now a popular tourist attraction.

Long popular in the US, Bushmills is now owned by Proximo Spirits, and Bushmills Original is matured in American oak casks.

Bottles to look out for:

Bushmills Original (ABV 40%)
Black Bush (ABV 40%)
Red Bush (ABV 40%)

IRELAND

Cooley

Location: County Louth

Key facts:

First founded in 1987 on the Cooley peninsula, Cooley distillery is now part of Suntory Holdings, and produces several specialist whiskeys including Connemara, a peated single malt, and The Tyrconnell®, a single malt.

The distillery has both column stills and copper pot stills.

Bottles to look out for:

Connemara Peated Single Malt Irish Whiskey (ABV 40%)
The Tyrconnell® Single Malt (ABV 43%)
Cooley 2002 19-year-old Rum Finish (ABV 53.8%)

IRELAND

Glendalough

Location: County Wicklow

Key facts:

An independent small distillery founded in 2011, Glendalough was founded by a group of friends who wanted to showcase small-batch Irish whiskey.

They installed a 500-litre Holstein still and like to experiment with different casks, for example in the Madeira Finish Single Cask expression (ABV 42%).

Bottles to look out for:

Glendalough Double Barrel Irish Whiskey (ABV 42%)
Glendalough Pot Still Irish Whiskey (ABV 43%)

IRELAND

Jameson

Location: County Cork

Key facts:

Jameson is the bestselling blended Irish whiskey on the global market, and has a long pedigree, having been founded in 1780.

Originally made in Dublin, it is now produced at the New Midleton Distillery in County Cork, which also makes other whiskeys including Powers, Paddy and Redbreast.

Bottles to look out for:

Jameson Original Irish Whiskey (ABV 40%)
Jameson Black Barrel (ABV 40%)
Jameson Crested (ABV 40%)
12-year-old Distillery Reserve (ABV 40%)

IRELAND

Tullamore Dew

Location: Tullamore, County Offaly

Key facts:

The original Tullamore distillery was founded in 1829, and its signature whiskey got the rest of its name from the initials of its creator, Daniel Edmund Williams.

When it was purchased by William Grant & Sons in 2010, a new distillery and visitor centre was built in Tullamore.

Bottles to look out for:

Tullamore Dew Irish Whiskey (ABV 40%)
Tullamore Dew 14-year-old Single Malt (ABV 41.3%)

USA

Buffalo Trace

Location: Frankfort, Kentucky

Key facts:

Formerly known as the George T. Stagg distillery, it was rebranded the Buffalo Trace distillery when its namesake brand was introduced in 1999.

The name refers to ancient paths carved out by buffalo that led the American pioneers through the wilderness.

Bottles to look out for:

Buffalo Trace (ABV 40%)
White Dog Mash No. 1 (ABV 62.5%)
Bourbon Cream (ABV 15%)

USA

Jack Daniel's

Location: Lynchburg, Tennessee

Key facts:

The oldest registered distillery in the US has been selling its distinctive square-shouldered bottles of Black Label whiskey for more than 140 years.

It is made from 80 per cent corn, 12 per cent rye and 8 per cent malted barley grains, and its maple-charcoal filtering process is its distinctive calling card.

Bottles to look out for:

Black Label (ABV 40%)
Gentleman Jack (ABV 40%)
Single Barrel Rye (ABV 47%)
Barrel Proof (ABV 62.5%)

USA

Jim Beam

Location: Clermont, Kentucky

Key facts:

One of the best-known bourbon brands, Jim Beam was consistently run by the Beam family from its founding in 1795 until its sale to Suntory Holdings in 2014.

The whiskey was originally called Old Tub before being renamed Jim Beam in 1943.

Bottles to look out for:

Jim Beam White Label (ABV 40%)
Jim Beam Black (ABV 45%)
Sunshine Blend (ABV 40%)

USA

Maker's Mark

Location: Loretto, Kentucky

Key facts:

A small-batch bourbon whisky (Maker's Mark is one of the few American distilleries that uses the Scottish spelling) that includes no rye in the mash, instead using red winter wheat, corn and malted barley.

It's aged for six years and is sold in squared bottles dipped in red wax, giving it a distinctive appearance.

Bottles to look out for:

Classic Maker's Mark (ABV 45%)
Maker's Mark No. 46 (ABV 47%)
Maker's Mark Cask Strength (ABV 55%)

USA

Michter's

Location: Originally Schaefferstown, Pennsylvania; now Louisville, Kentucky

Key facts:

Michter's celebrates its long heritage on the old-style label: founded in 1753 by John Shenk, it has changed hands many times, and eventually got its name from the sons of the distiller, Michael and Peter Forman.

Bottles to look out for:

US*1 Kentucky Straight Bourbon (ABV 45.7%)
Unblended American Whiskey (ABV 41.7%)

USA

WhistlePig

Location: Shoreham, Vermont

Key facts:

Known for its premium rye whiskey, WhistlePig was founded in 2007 by entrepreneur Raj Bhakta, and released its first ten-year-old rye in 2015.

Its lead distiller and chief blender are both women, unusually in the industry, and the name derives from the Kunekune pigs that live on site.

Bottles to look out for:

PiggyBack Rye (ABV 48.28%)
PiggyBack Bourbon (ABV 48.28%)

USA

Woodford Reserve

Location: Woodford County, Kentucky

Key facts:

A small-batch premium bourbon made from a combination of copper pot still spirits and column still spirits.

The distillery was formerly known as the Old Oscar Pepper Distillery before the Woodford Reserve spirit was launched to great success in 1996.

Bottles to look out for:

Woodford Reserve Bourbon (ABV 45.2%)
Woodford Reserve Double Oaked (ABV 43.2%)
Chocolate Whisper Redux Bourbon (ABV 69.7%)

CANADA

Bearface

Location: near Nasko,
northern British Columbia

Key facts:

This small distillery uses a process they call elemental ageing, in which varied casks are exposed to the north Canadian climate and steep temperature fluctuations.

The distillery likes to innovate unusual styles of whisky not found elsewhere, such as its One Eleven blend.

Bottles to look out for:

Bearface Triple Oak (ABV 42.5%)
The One Eleven Series (ABV 42.5%)

CANADA

Canadian Mist

Location: Collingwood, Ontario

Key facts:

Canadian Mist is a triple-distilled blend of several grain whiskies (barley, corn and rye) known for a light, balanced flavour profile.

It was created in 1967 in Georgian Bay, Ontario, but is now owned by the Sazerac company and is bottled and distributed from Louisville, Kentucky.

Popular in the US, it's great for classic cocktails.

Bottles to look out for:

Canadian Mist (ABV 40%)

CANADA

Crown Royal

Location: Gimli, Manitoba

Key facts:

First created in 1939 to mark the royal visit of King George VI, Crown Royal blended whisky has since become the most popular Canadian whisky in the US, partly thanks to its distinctive appearance and purple velvet bag.

Said to be a blend of 50 different whiskies, it was originally owned by Seagram's, and now by Diageo.

Bottles to look out for:

Flavoured versions (such as Crown Royal Peach, Vanilla or Apple) (ABV 40%)
Crown Royal Reserve (ABV 40%)
Crown Royal Black (ABV 40%)

CANADA

Hiram Walker & Sons

Location: Windsor, Ontario

Key facts:

Hiram Walker founded the distillery in the mid-nineteenth century, and set up Walkerville, a model community for his employees.

The biggest distillery in North America, it produces Canadian Club (known as CC), perhaps the most iconic Canadian whisky brand, which is sold worldwide, as well as other small-batch brands.

Bottles to look out for:

Canadian Club 1858 (ABV 40%)
Lot 40 Rye Whisky (ABV 43%)
18-year-old J.P. Wiser's (ABV 40%)
10-year-old Pike Creek (ABV 42%)

CANADA

Macaloney's Island Distillery

Location: Saanich, British Columbia

Key facts:

The distillery was founded in 2016 by Graeme Macaloney and uses Forsyth's copper pot stills with Canadian barley and oak casks sourced from all around the world to produce high-end single malts.

Their Peat Project Moscatel Barrique Single Malt (ABV 50%) won Whisky of the Year at the 2025 Canadian Whisky Awards.

Bottles to look out for:

Macaloney's Peat Project (ABV 46%)
Island Drams (ABV 46%)

JAPAN

Chichibu

Location: Chichibu, Saitama prefecture

Key facts:

Chichibu rose out of the ashes of the celebrated Hanyu distillery in 2004, when it was founded by Ichiro Akuto, sometimes called the "whisky wizard".

It is a small-batch distillery that has a cult following, makes its own whisky barrels on site and has prices to match.

Bottles to look out for:

Chichibu Red Wine Cask 2023 (ABV 50.5%)
10-year-old Chichibu (ABV 50.5%)

JAPAN

Chugoku Jozo

Location: Hiroshima prefecture

Key facts:

Originally founded to make sake, the Chugoku distillery switched to whisky production and developed its signature Togouchi blended whisky, made from imported Scotch whisky and locally produced whisky.

It is aged in the Togouchi Tunnel, originally built for the railway, where the cool, humid atmosphere means it ages slowly and takes on a smooth, refined character.

Bottles to look out for:

12- and 18-year-old Togouchi (both ABV 43%)

JAPAN

Nikka

Location: Several locations

Key facts:

The Nikka Whisky Distilling Co owns the Yoichi distillery in Hokkaido, and the Miyagikyo distillery in Sendai, Miyagi prefecture.

Nikka's innovative Coffey still uses indirect steam to heat the grain, allowing the flavours to persist. Established in 1934 by Masataka Taketsuru, the company combines traditional Scottish know-how with Japanese craftsmanship.

Bottles to look out for:

Nikka Coffey Grain Whisky (ABV 45%)
Nikka Whisky From The Barrel (ABV 51.4%)
Individual single malt releases

JAPAN

Suntory Hakushu

Location: Yamanashi prefecture

Key facts:

Known as the "mountain forest" distillery, the Hakushu distillery is located in the southern Japanese Alps, an area famous for the quality of its water.

It produces gentler whiskies than Yamazaki, using washbacks made from local wood that give the whiskies a unique character.

Bottles to look out for:

Hakushu Distiller's Reserve Single Malt (ABV 43%)

JAPAN

Suntory Yamazaki

Location: Shimamoto, Osaka prefecture

Key facts:

Founded by Shinjiro Torii in 1923, the venerable Yamazaki distillery, near Mount Tennozan, southwest of Kyoto, was purchased by Suntory and now produces Suntory's flagship single malt, aged in American, Spanish and Japanese Mizunara Oak.

It was the first single malt distillery in Japan.

Bottles to look out for:

Yamazaki Distiller's Reserve (ABV 43%)
12-, 18- and 25-year-old Reserves (all ABV 43%)

JAPAN

White Oak Distillery

Location: Akashi, Hyogo prefecture

Key facts:

Using pot stills and oak casks, the White Oak distillery combines traditional approaches with Japanese innovation, quality control and precision.

The oak referred to in the name features prominently in the flavours of vanilla and caramel.

It's part of the Akashi Sake Brewery.

Bottles to look out for:

White Oak Akashi Blended Whisky (ABV 40%)
Single Malts (ABV 46%)

INDIA

Amrut Whisky Distillery

Location: Bangalore

Key facts:

Amrut was established in 1948, and began producing malt whisky in the 1980s.

Its whiskies are made with barley grown in the foothills of the Himalayas and, because of the hot climate, mature very rapidly.

They tend to feature citrus and big fruit flavours.

Bottles to look out for:

Amrut Fusion (ABV 50%)
Amrut Peated Cask Strength (ABV 62.8%)

CHINA

Goalong Distillery

Location: Hunan

Key facts:

Located in the south of China, Goalong's single malt and blended whiskies were the first in the country to be exported overseas.

Goalong whiskies feature floral notes along with fruit, hazelnut and honey.

Bottles to look out for:

Goalong 5-year-old Bourbon Cask Single Malt (ABV 40%)
Goalong Blended Whiskey (ABV 40%)

SOUTH AFRICA

James Sedgwick Distillery

Location: Wellington

Key facts:

The only commercial distillery in Africa, James Sedgwick has been distilling since 1886, producing award-winning single malts and grains as well as blends.

The African climate allows for fast maturation and the development of rich, spicy flavour profiles.

Bottles to look out for:

Three Ships 12-year-old Single Malt (ABV 46.3%)
Bain's Cape Mountain Single Grain (ABV 40%)

UK

The English Distillery

Location: Thetford, Norfolk

Key facts:

When it was set up in 2006, the English Distillery was the first whisky distillery in England for over a century.

Using English barley, yeast and water, the distillery produces both peated and unpeated whiskies with notes of vanilla and spice.

Bottles to look out for:

The English Original (ABV 43%)
The English Smokey (ABV 43%)

DENMARK

Stauning

Location: Stauning, West Jutland

Key facts:

Set up by a group of friends in an old slaughterhouse, Stauning Distillery began in 2005 and has already gained international acclaim.

Using local grains and peats, and many varieties of casks, Stauning puts a distinctively Danish twist on whisky drinking.

Bottles to look out for:

Stauning HØST Double Malt Whisky (ABV 40.5%)
Stauning Bastard Rye Whisky Mezcal Finish (ABV 46.3%)

AUSTRALIA

Sullivan's Cove

Location: Hobart, Tasmania

Key facts:

This distillery makes the most of Tasmania's Scotland-like climate and uses traditional small-batch production methods and pot stills with ex-bourbon barrels.

It produces a range of whiskies, including single malts and single casks, and the whisky-making team enjoys experimenting with ageing in different barrels.

The whiskies command high prices.

Bottles to look out for:

French Oak Single Cask (ABV 47.5%)
Double Cask (ABV 46.9%)

Chapter Three
How to Drink It
Getting the Best From Your Dram

"I like to drink. I like to drink good whiskey. But I'm not one of those people who drink whiskey in a fancy glass. A bottle is good enough for me."

William Faulkner,
***The Sound and the Fury* (1929)**

HOW TO SERVE WHISKY

Although whisky purists will tell you that there's only one way to drink whisky – straight up and unadorned – in reality, many people prefer a well-chosen addition to help them enjoy their favourite dram.

Adding a small amount of water can help the flavours and aromas to unfurl a little, and ice cubes can have a similar effect, but it's harder to control how much they dilute the drink.

Ice can also help you identify strong flavours more easily and can counteract the alcohol "burn", but it also affects the mouthfeel.

Spherical 2½-inch (6-cm) ice balls are now popular, which chill, but do not dilute, the drink.

WHISKEY MIXERS

In general, American and Irish whiskeys are more likely to be drunk with a mixer, and Scotch single malts without. But several Scottish distilleries have signature blends designed to be drunk this way, such as Johnnie Walker Red Label.

SODA WATER

Scotch and soda is 1 part whisky to 2 parts soda water.

SPARKLING MINERAL WATER

The whisky highball, which is especially popular in Japan, is 1 part whisky to 2 or 3 parts sparkling water in a tall tumbler, served over ice with a slice of lemon.

GINGER ALE OR GINGER BEER

Ginger beer's stronger flavour may mask a really good whisky.

GINGER WINE

A Whisky *Mac*, equal parts whisky and ginger wine, is a good winter warmer after a long day.

WHISKY TASTING

To assess a whisky, there are five stages that professionals go through. These can really help you savour and appreciate the liquid in the glass.

1. LOOK AT THE COLOUR

Usually, the longer it has been aged, the darker it is, and the type of barrel can affect the colour too. Some cheaper whiskies add colourings to their whisky, so a darker colour does not always mean better or more flavour.

2. SWIRL THE WHISKY AROUND IN THE GLASS

As the liquid returns to the bottom it leaves trails, or "legs" down the side of the glass. The faster these descend, the lighter the body of the whisky; full-bodied whiskies with an oilier, thicker mouthfeel have legs that descend more slowly.

3. "NOSE" THE WHISKY BY SMELLING IT

At first the strongest impression will come from alcohol vapours, but soon the aromas will start to emerge. Opening your mouth slightly helps your olfactory system.

4. TASTE IT

Allow the whisky to spread all around your palate and coat your mouth before swallowing or spitting. As well as flavours, you may notice the mouthfeel or texture of the whisky; some have more viscosity than others.

5. FINALLY, CONSIDER THE FINISH

This is the lasting impression of the whisky after you have swallowed it. Different flavours can emerge, and the sensations can last different amounts of time.

WHISKY TASTING NOTES

FRUIT

Perhaps you taste pear, apple, peach, pineapple or banana flavours, which appear during fermenting and distilling. Some people may experience these more as acetone (nail varnish remover). Dried fruit or raisin notes can come from the cask.

CEREAL

Cereal, malty or toasty notes come from how the barley or other grain is roasted and evolve during the mashing and fermentation stages.

WOOD & SPICE

These normally come from the casks the whisky is aged in, and can include vanilla, coconut, clove, pine or toasty flavours.

SMOKE/CHEMICAL

The peat used to roast the barley determines these flavours, which can include smokiness, tar, TCP, bonfires, petrol, lapsang souchong tea and coal.

GRASSY/FLORAL

Fresh-cut grass, wildflowers, violets, honey and moss-like notes come from the fermenting and distillation process.

OTHERS

Other aromas that can be detected in some whiskies, and which may be considered undesirable depending on consumer preference, include sulphur, cheesiness, rotten eggs and onions.

Amber Moon

This whisky variant of the classic frontier pick-me-up cocktail, the Prairie Oyster, is said to be the ideal hangover cure.

INGREDIENTS

1 small egg yolk
1 tsp malt vinegar
1 tsp tomato ketchup
1 dash Worcestershire sauce
2 dashes Tabasco sauce
2 tbsp (30 ml) whisky

- Place the egg yolk in a chilled cocktail glass.
- Stir the vinegar, ketchup, Worcestershire sauce and Tabasco with ice until chilled.
- Carefully strain the mixture over the egg yolk.
- Slowly pour the whisky on top to create a layer and drink immediately.

Jack Daniel's is a corn-based, aged Tennessee whiskey (technically a type of bourbon), and the maple syrup is great with its slightly smoky undertones, the result of the whiskey being filtered through maple charcoal.

Jumpin' Jack Daniel's

You can make this with regular bourbon or even rye whiskey instead, if you like.

INGREDIENTS

2 fl oz (60 ml) Jack Daniel's or other bourbon whiskey
1 tsp maple syrup
2 tbsp (30 ml) sweet red vermouth
2 dashes bitters, such as Angostura (optional)
Strip of lemon zest, to garnish

- Fill a short tumbler with ice cubes and pour in the Jack Daniel's, maple syrup, vermouth and bitters. Stir well for at least 5 seconds.
- Twist the lemon zest strip over the top of the drink and drop it in.

Kentucky Bloody Mary

This Bloody Mary with a Southern twist uses bourbon or rye whiskey, instead of the usual vodka, to add a delicious, sweet smokiness, which is bolstered by the paprika.

INGREDIENTS

2 fl oz (60 ml) bourbon or rye whiskey
3½ fl oz (100 ml) tomato juice
1 tbsp lemon juice, freshly squeezed
8 dashes Tabasco
4 dashes Worcestershire sauce
Freshly ground black pepper and celery salt, to taste (optional)
Sweet smoked paprika, to taste
Lemon wedge, to garnish

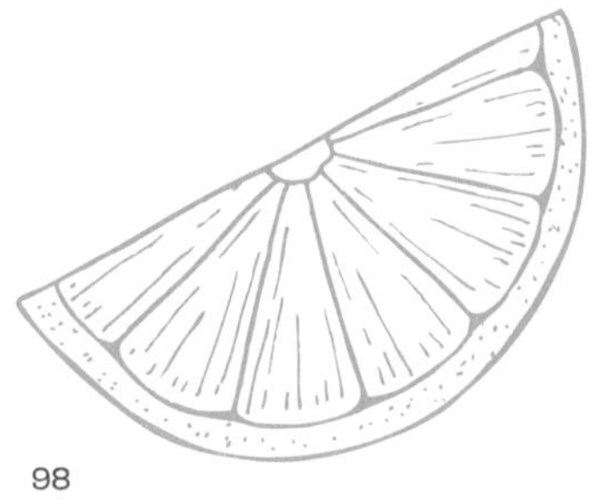

- Fill a large tumbler or hurricane glass with ice.
- Fill a cocktail shaker with ice cubes and pour in the bourbon or rye whiskey, tomato juice, lemon juice, Tabasco and Worcestershire sauce.
- Add a grind of black pepper and a pinch of celery salt (if using). Then add a generous pinch of smoked paprika.
- Shake well for at least 10 seconds, then strain into the ice-filled glass.
- Garnish with the lemon wedge and sprinkle with a little more smoked paprika.

The vermouth used determines whether it's a Dry Manhattan (dry vermouth, no cherry), a Sweet Manhattan (Italian vermouth and a cherry) or a Perfect Manhattan (half dry, half sweet vermouth).

Manhattan

Authentic Manhattans were originally made with the rye whiskey beloved of true New Yorkers.

INGREDIENTS

2 fl oz (60 ml) bourbon or rye whiskey
2 tbsp dry or sweet Italian vermouth
Dash of Angostura bitters
Orange zest and maraschino cherry, to garnish

- Stir the bourbon or whiskey, vermouth and bitters with ice in a cocktail shaker.
- Strain into a chilled glass.
- Spritz over the orange zest and drop it in, then add the cherry.

Mint Julep

Try using other types of whiskey and experimenting with the amount of sugar syrup to find the version you like best.

INGREDIENTS

10–12 fresh mint leaves, plus a sprig to garnish
2 tsp sugar syrup
2 fl oz (60 ml) bourbon or other whiskey
Dash of Angostura bitters (optional)

- Use a muddler (a blunt tool like a pestle) to lightly crush the mint leaves with the sugar syrup in a chilled julep cup or glass.
- Add the bourbon and the bitters, if using.
- Stir well and fill the glass with crushed ice.
- Garnish with a sprig of mint, more ice and a straw.

The classic mint julep originated in 19th-century America, and remains a fantastic drink for a hot day.

Described by some cocktail experts as the "primordial drink", the Old Fashioned (originally the Old Fashioned Whiskey Cocktail) first appeared around 1806.

Old Fashioned

Like several of the very oldest cocktails, there are many variations, and bartenders still debate the best way to make it.

INGREDIENTS

2 fl oz (60 ml) bourbon or rye whiskey
1 tsp sugar syrup
Dash of Angostura bitters
Orange zest and maraschino cherry, to garnish

- Pour half the whiskey or bourbon into a chilled glass with the sugar syrup and a couple of ice cubes. Stir well until fully combined.
- Add the rest of the whiskey and the bitters with more ice and stir again thoroughly.
- Spritz the orange zest over and drop it in. Garnish with a maraschino cherry.

Rob Roy

A Rob Roy is a bit like a Negroni or a Manhattan, but with a subtler bitterness and the whisky flavours shining through.

INGREDIENTS

2 fl oz (60 ml) Scotch whisky
2 tbsp red vermouth
A few dashes of Angostura bitters
Strip of orange zest
Maraschino cherry, to garnish (optional)

- Pour the whisky, vermouth and bitters into a cocktail shaker filled with ice cubes and stir well until very cold.
- Fill a short tumbler with ice cubes and strain the cocktail over.
- Twist the orange zest over the drink and drop it in, then add the cherry to garnish (if using).

Sometimes the simplest combinations are the best, and this one is great for showcasing a really special whisky.

This absolute classic is great for introducing people to whisky if they're not sure whether they like it.

Rusty Nail

A lovely after-dinner drink which is super-simple to put together.

INGREDIENTS

2 fl oz (60 ml) Scotch whisky

1 tbsp Drambuie, Stag's Breath, Jack Daniel's Tennessee Honey or other honey-flavoured whisky liqueur

Strip of lemon zest

- Fill a tumbler with ice cubes.
- Pour over the whisky and Drambuie and stir well until cold.
- Twist the lemon zest over the drink and drop it in.

Rye of the Tiger

This light, fruity number is perfect for channelling 1980s glamour, and is definitely an excuse to get out your fanciest cocktail glasses, straws, stirrers or cocktail umbrellas. The egg white provides a luxurious, silky texture, but you can easily leave it out.

INGREDIENTS

1 fresh strawberry, chopped, plus ½ strawberry to garnish
2 fl oz (60 ml) rye whiskey
1 tbsp Cointreau or triple sec
2 tsp grenadine
1½ tbsp crème de fraise
1 tbsp freshly squeezed lemon juice
½ egg white (optional)

- Put the strawberry in a cocktail shaker and muddle it to extract as much juice as possible.
- Add a generous handful of ice cubes, then pour in the rye whiskey, Cointreau, grenadine, crème de fraise, lemon juice and egg white (if using).
- Put the lid on and shake well for at least 10 seconds.
- Double-strain into a cocktail glass and garnish with a strawberry half.

The classic Sazerac cocktail originated in 1850s New Orleans, and comprised Cognac, sugar and Peychaud's bitters. Later, rye whiskey or bourbon were often substituted when Cognac supplies were running low – and they are great additions.

Sazerac

INGREDIENTS

2 tbsp bourbon or rye whiskey
2 tbsp Cognac
2 tsp sugar syrup
2 dashes of bitters (preferably Peychaud's or Angostura)
Lemon zest, to garnish (optional)

- Pour all ingredients bar the garnish into a cocktail shaker and stir with ice cubes until very cold.
- Strain into a short tumbler or rocks glass.
- Spritz the lemon zest over the drink and drop it in.

Scotch-52

This whisky-inspired version of the infamous B-52 shooter celebrates whisky alongside two of its most beloved spin-offs: Baileys and Drambuie.

INGREDIENTS

1 tbsp Baileys Irish Cream
1 tbsp Drambuie
1 tbsp Scotch whisky

- Slowly and carefully pour the ingredients in the order listed into a chilled tall shot glass to form layers.
- Pouring each one slowly over the back of a teaspoon helps to keep the layers separate.

"There is no bad whiskey. There are only some whiskeys that aren't as good as others."

Raymond Chandler (1888–1959)

Twisted Whisky Highball

This orange-scented whiskey twist on the rock 'n' roll classic, rum and Coke, will get your evening off to a great start.

INGREDIENTS

2 fl oz (60 ml) Irish whiskey or bourbon
2 tbsp dark rum
1 tbsp Cointreau or triple sec
3 dashes orange bitters (optional)
Coke, well-chilled, to top
Strip of orange zest, to garnish

- Half-fill a tall tumbler or highball glass with ice cubes.
- Pour in the whiskey, rum, orange liqueur and bitters, if using, and stir well for 5 seconds.
- Add a handful more ice cubes and top with Coke.
- Twist the orange zest strip over the top and drop it into the drink.

Whisky & Ginger Refresher

This delicious whisky and ginger number is great as a pick-me-up at any time of day, but especially before or after dinner. Add a slice of fresh ginger if you like it extra fiery.

INGREDIENTS

2½ tbsp blended Scotch whisky
2 tbsp ginger liqueur
1 tsp runny honey
Ginger beer, well-chilled, to top

- Fill a cocktail shaker with ice cubes.
- Add the whisky, ginger liqueur and honey, put the lid on the shaker and shake for at least 10 seconds.
- Strain into an ice-filled tumbler and top with ginger beer.

"What whisky will not cure, there is no cure for."

Old Irish proverb

The Cuba Libre, which is made with rum, was born in a bar in Havana in 1900, when a customer ordered a rum and coke with lime juice and proposed a toast – "Por Cuba Libre!" – to celebrate Cuba's recently won independence from Spain. Swapping the rum for whiskey makes an intriguing combination.

Whiskey Libre

INGREDIENTS

2 lime wedges, plus 1 extra to garnish
Dash of Angostura bitters (optional)
2 fl oz (60 ml) bourbon or rye whiskey
Coke, to top

- Fill a glass with ice cubes, squeeze over the lime wedges and drop them in.
- Add the bitters, if using, and the bourbon, then stir well.
- Top with Coke, stir gently and garnish with an extra wedge of lime.

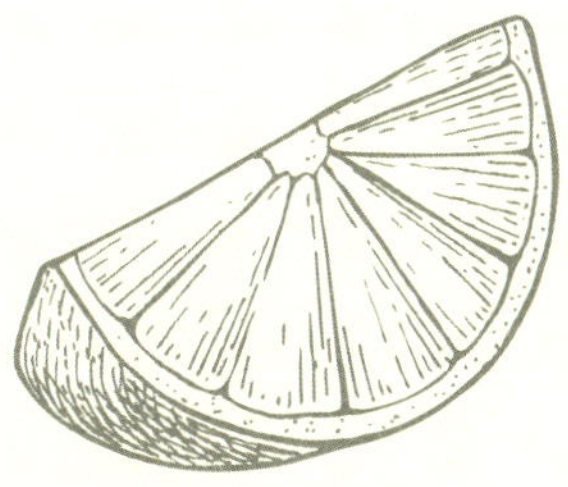

Whisky Martini

Use your best martini glass, make sure it's ice cold, then sit back and turn up the volume.

INGREDIENTS

2½ tbsp gin
2 tbsp blended Scotch whisky, such as Johnnie Walker Red Label
1 tbsp sweet red vermouth
Olive, to garnish

- Fill a cocktail shaker with ice cubes.
- Pour in the gin, whisky and vermouth and stir well for at least 10 seconds.
- Strain into a chilled martini glass and garnish with an olive.

Including a dash of whisky in a sweet martini adds a delicious hint of caramel smokiness that truly suits it.

In 1947, Orson Welles aptly summed up the appeal of the negroni:

"The bitters are excellent for your liver, the gin is bad for you. They balance each other."

Whisky Negroni

This version of a negroni swaps gin for whisky.

INGREDIENTS

2 tbsp whisky
2 tbsp Campari
2 tbsp sweet red vermouth
Orange zest, to garnish

- Stir the ingredients together in a chilled glass filled with ice.
- Spritz the orange zest over the drink and drop it in.

Whisky Sour

In this recipe, egg white can be omitted, but it's well worth trying for the silky mouthfeel it brings.

INGREDIENTS

2 fl oz (60 ml) whiskey or whisky
1½ tbsp freshly squeezed lemon juice
1–2 tbsp sugar syrup
Dash of egg white (optional)
Dash of Angostura bitters (optional)
Lemon slice and maraschino cherry, to garnish

- Shake all the ingredients in a cocktail shaker with ice, then strain into an ice-filled glass, ideally a short tumbler.
- Garnish with a slice of lemon and a cherry.

The Sour – basically spirit + lemon juice + sugar – is one of the oldest cocktail formulas.

The whiskey (or whisky) version was first mentioned in print in 1870, making it one of the oldest and most venerable recipes.

“Drinking whiskey is like giving a gift to yourself.”

Billy Collins,
***The Art of Drowning* (1995)**